10 Psalms For Petty People Like Me

Suncera Johnson

Words to Live By Publishing

10 Psalms for Petty People Like Me

First edition

Copyright © 2021 by Suncera Johnson

All Scripture quotations are taken from *THE MESSAGE*, copyright © 1993, 2002, 2018 by Eugene H. Peterson. Used by permission of NavPress. All rights reserved. Represented by Tyndale House Publishers, a Division of Tyndale House Ministries

10 Psalms for Petty People Like Me

ISBN: 978-1-7351596-3-8

Printed in the United States of America

CONTENTS

INTRODUCTION

WHY PETTY?

I didn't write this book to make a mockery of prayer. I wrote this book because I realize that there are times that I ask God to do things that I know are not of his will. There are times that I ask God for revenge that isn't mine to give. And I know I am not alone.

In reading the Psalms through the lens of various bible translations, I realized that the Psalmists had days like we all do – those times when we get petty. And in our feelings.

I chose my ten favorite "Petty Psalms" and allowed them to guide me in fully expressing how I feel to God.

I hope this book helps you to do the same.

PSALM 19:13

Clean the slate, God, so we can start the day fresh! Keep me from stupid sins, from thinking I can take over your work; Then I can start this day sun-washed, scrubbed clean of the grime of sin.

Overthinking.
It's what I do.
It's my greatest struggle.
It feeds my insecurities.
It feeds my fears.
And it cripples my faith.
It produces anxiety.
And it thrives in "what ifs".
I seek answers to questions
long before I should.
I seek answers to questions
that have no answer.
It is difficult for me to just be.
I've learned that there is a
name for the stupid sin
I find myself caught up in
more frequently than I desire;
It's called anticipatory fear.
I borrow trouble from
tomorrow that does not exist.
In my mind, it's real.
My body reacts.
The panic.
The anxiety.
And the need to DO something.
But this stupid sin of mine is
diminishing in its hold on me.

With each passing day, its
power lessens with the lessons.
And instead, my faith is
continuing to grow.
And my growing faith starves
my weakening insecurities.
And my growing faith evicts
my weakening fears.
And that is why today, and
every day
that I lay this stupid sin of
mine before you in prayer,
I can start the day fresh!

What is your stupid sin?

PSALM 6:1-2

Please, God, no more yelling,
no more trips to the
woodshed.
Treat me nice for a change;

I get it.
You disciple those you love.
We reap what we sow.
There are consequences for our
disobedience.
But, God if you love us as much
as you say you do,
Why does it seem like
sometimes you let the
suffering
Continue just a little while
longer.
When we know you could take
it all away?
It's like the parent who yells
incessantly at a child.
And constantly reminds us of
our bad behavior.
Except that you use
circumstances in our lives
That regurgitate a piercing yell
when we are reminded
Of what we should have or
should not have done.
In your love, can't you just
make it go away?
Can't you move the clock

backward so we can get a do over?
Can't you move the clock forward so we can get past this season?
Can't you just remove us from all of the things in our lives right now
That cause us grief?
Do you want to see us suffer?
We know the answer:
You love us just as we are, but love us too much to let us remain the same.
So, even in the piercing consequences of our lives,
Whether as a result of our actions
Or those of others,
Can you do us a solid?
Show us some mercy, grace and favor?
And get us out of here?

What circumstances do you want God to rescue you from?

_____

_____

_____

_____

_____

_____

_____

_____

_____

_____

_____

_____

_____

_____

_____

_____

PSALM 17:4

I'm not trying to get my way
in the world's way.
I'm trying to get your way,
your Word's way.

I'm really trying to get this thing right, God.
I know I'm not perfect.
But I am really doing the best I can.
It seems that no matter what I do,
I can't seem to get it right.
My motives get twisted.
People assume things about me
that just are not true.
And all I want to do is be Obedient.
To your will, your plan and your purpose for my life.
It's not about money.
It's not about fame.
It's not about recognition.
It's not about me at all.
It is all about who you have called me to be.
And what you have called me to do.
So, please protect me.
Protect me from my ego.

Protect me from those who
hate me.
Protect me from those who are
envious of me.
And Lord, protect me from
those
who want to be me.
Reveal those who are enemies
Disguised as friends.
And remove those who are
Constantly seeking ways
To put me down.

What obstacles are you facing in relationships while seeking God's will for your life?

_____

_____

_____

_____

_____

_____

_____

_____

_____

_____

_____

_____

_____

_____

_____

_____

_____

PSALM 34:13

Guard your tongue from
profanity,
and no more lying through
your teeth.

Sometimes, I lie. I'm not a liar,
per se.
But, sometimes I bend the
truth
Albeit ever so slightly.
I mean, it doesn't hurt anyone,
or so it seems.
And there are times when it
feels as if the only words
that will suffice are profane.
When my anger has boiled over
to the point of rage,
I might say a few things that
while
Temporarily releasing my
anger
Leave me feeling guilty
afterwards.
Whether it's a lie or profanity.
Can you work on my tongue,
God?
Truth be told,
I want to be honest but
sometimes omission
simply does not feel like lying.

And cursing, feels like the only
way to get through to some
people.
But if it distances me from you,
Is it really worth it?
So, help me.
I want my tongue, heart, mind
and soul
To reflect my love for you.
And in those moments when it
Seems as I have no other
alternative,
Please bring this verse to my
mind.
And send help.
Transform my spirit.
Cause my anger to subside.
And help me so that
I don't feel backed into any
Corners that will imprison me
In a cage of lies.

Which lies are the easiest for you to tell?

_____

_____

_____

_____

_____

_____

_____

_____

_____

_____

_____

_____

_____

_____

_____

_____

_____

_____

PSALM 56:5-6

They don't let up—
they smear my reputation
and huddle to plot my
collapse.
They gang up,
sneak together through the
alleys
To take me by surprise,
wait their chance to get me.

As hard as it is to accept
some people simply want to
see me fail.
I'm not paranoid, Lord.
Because I have watched it
happen.
Their cunning,
calculating,
manipulation,
posing as a friend.
When they are actually the
enemy.
Secretly seeking to plot against
me.
I cannot comprehend
Why one person thinks they
need to step on the shoulders
of another
In order to raise themselves
up.
Can't we walk up the ladder
Side by side in honesty?
Why do they say things about
me
In secret, that they would
never
Say to my face?

Can you get at them God?
Because I don't need this in my
life.
I want to focus on what you
have planned for me to do.
More so than on the
anticipation
Of the ruin that others
Are plotting against me.

Who is the biggest human opposition currently plotting against you?

_____

_____

_____

_____

_____

_____

_____

_____

_____

_____

_____

_____

_____

_____

_____

_____

PSALM 109:7-8

When he's judged, let the
verdict be "Guilty",
and when he prays, let his
prayer turn to sin.
Give him a short life,
and give his job to somebody
else.

We often hear that
Hurt people, hurt people.
God, that does not
make me feel
any better
about the pain
inflicted upon me.
I want to see them suffer
For the way they have treated
me
And how I have felt as a result.
I know vengeance is yours,
But that is little consolation
when it
Looks like my accusers
Are prospering.
Getting away with everything.
Incurring consequences for
nothing.
And continuing to be a source
Of turmoil in my life.
I want to see them suffer.
And I know you can do it.
Because you have the power to.
And I know you answer my
prayers.
But help me to be careful God.

Because these seeds I plant
With words.
Will multiply.
And be scattered.
And who is to say that
everything that
I wish upon my enemy
Will not manifest as fruit in my
own life?

Who do you need to forgive?

_____

_____

_____

_____

_____

_____

_____

_____

_____

_____

_____

_____

_____

_____

_____

_____

_____

_____

PSALM 52:3-4

You love evil more than good,
you call black white.
You love malicious gossip,
you foul-mouth.

I listen to how they talk about
others
To me.
I often wonder if they hear
what they
Are saying
Or understand
What they are really
communicating to me?
If they lie about others,
If they tell me all of someone
else's business,
What are they saying about me
When I am not around?
Isn't that what foul-mouthed
gossipers do?
They love to talk about the bad.
And act like they have
something good to share.
As if juicy is a measure of what
I want to hear.
I'm not perfect.
I talk about the imperfections
of others as well.
Am I like them?
Do I get pleasure in discussing
the failure of others?

What if I am more like them
Than I care to admit.
What if someone else is
reading this and thinking these
words
Also apply to me?
Can I really be trusted?
Am I simply a hypocrite hiding
behind my words?

What harmful conversations do you need to stop?

PSALM 13:3-4

Take a good look at me, God,
my God;
I want to look life in the eye,
So no enemy can get the best
of me
or laugh when I fall on my
face.

Some days I am unsure
Who to trust, What to say,
When to stop, Where to go,
Or why I should do anything at
all.
I want to be whole.
But is that really possible?
Praying it away just does not
work, God.
Even the Bible says
Absent of work, Faith is dead.
So how do I live?
What should I do now? What
should I do next?
Because I often feel like
The eyes of the world
Are watching me.
It could be my family,
It might be friends,
It might be competitors in
business,
Or coworkers
But it's hard to balance
striving to succeed
When I am afraid of what
others
Will think when I fail.

Do you have my back?
Can I trust you, God?
I need to know
That whether I am taking
giant leaps of faith
or tiptoeing through daily life
that you can trust me
with what you have given me
to do.
As much as I am surrendering
my trust to you.

What would you do today if you were not afraid?

_____

_____

_____

_____

_____

_____

_____

_____

_____

_____

_____

_____

_____

_____

_____

_____

_____

PSALM 56:8

You've kept track of my every
toss and turn
through the sleepless nights,
Each tear entered in your
ledger,
each ache written in your
book.

You already know God.
Although it feels like I am
alone.
Shedding tears in silence
Which pool in my pillow
as others sleep peacefully
you know every tear I have
shed.
No need to humiliate myself
pouring my heart out to
Those who do not care.
Those so consumed by their
own pain
they cannot bear to learn of
mine
nor are able to process
this pain writhing in my soul.
Yet, there you are.
Taking notes.
Not just of things as they
happen.
But in my private time.
In the hidden places of my
heart
When I cry inside
While smiling on the outside,
Hoping that the tears will stop.

All the while knowing
All things will work out for my
good.
Because I love you.
Even as my heart breaks,
I respect the process.
And I turn to you.
Because you know all of my
secrets.
And the tears upon which they
float.

What has caused tears to stain your pillow?

_____

_____

_____

_____

_____

_____

_____

_____

_____

_____

_____

_____

_____

_____

_____

PSALM 32:5

Then I let it all out;
I said, I'll make a clean
breast of my failures to God.
Suddenly the pressure was
gone—
my guilt dissolved,
my sin disappeared.

Only you, Lord.
Can obliterate the shame of my
failures.
Only you, Father.
Can love me in spite of
Me deserving a guilty verdict.
Only you, Savior.
Can forgive me
unconditionally.
Over and over again.
You are always there
With open arms.
Waiting to embrace me
When I would rather escape
The consequences of
My action or inaction.
The results of decisions
I made or did not make
And now today.
I am ready
To give it all to you
And accept that you alone
Can handle it all.
As I breathe a deep sigh of
relief
Letting every hindrance fall
behind me

Can you remind me of this
When guilt, shame and fear
Crouch at my door
Seeking to linger in my heart?

What failure do you need to release today?

Visit lifestylebysuncera.com
to learn more about the
author.